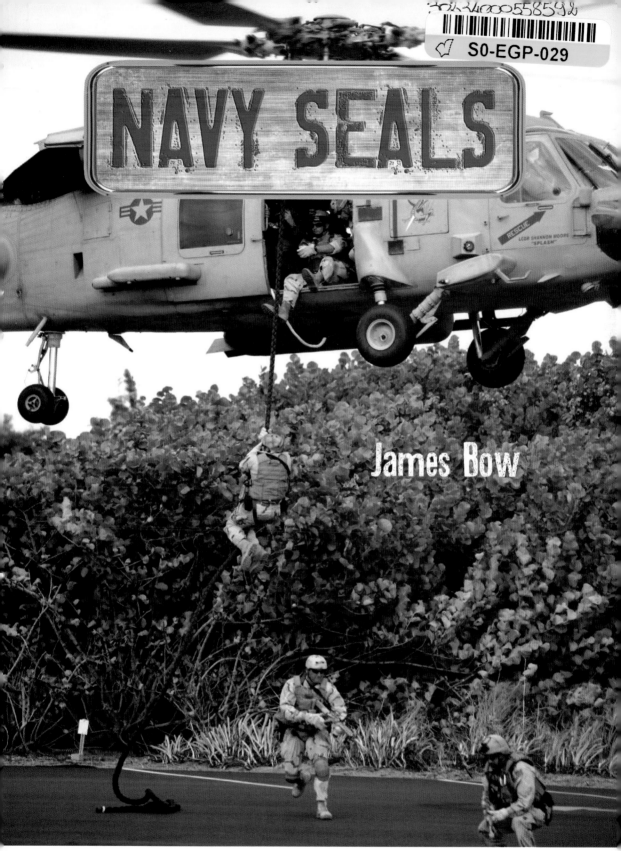

NAVY SEALS

James Bow

Crabtree Publishing Company

www.crabtreebooks.com

Crabtree Publishing Company

www.crabtreebooks.com

Author: James Bow
Publishing plan research and development:
   Sean Charlebois, Reagan Miller
   Crabtree Publishing Company
Photo research: Rachel Minay/
   Sonya Newland
Editors: Rachel Minay, Kathy Middleton
Design: Tim Mayer (Mayer Media)
Cover design: Ken Wright
Production and print coordinator:
   Katherine Berti
Prepress technician: Katherine Berti

Produced for Crabtree Publishing by
White-Thomson Publishing

Reading levels determined by
Publishing Solutions Group.
Content level: P
Readability level: L

Photographs:
Corbis: pp. 18–19; Bettmann: p. 8; Louie
Psihoyos: pp. 6–7; Peter Souza/White
House/Handout/The White House: pp.
42–43; S. SABAWOON/epa: pp. 26–27;
DefenseImagery.Mil: James Woods: pp.
22–23; JO1 Robert Benson: p. 20; MC2 Kyle
D. Gahlau: pp. 14–15; MC2 Shauntae
Hinkle-Lymas: pp. 10, 12–13; MCCS
Jeremy L. Wood: pp. 4–5; SGT Daniel P.
Shook: pp. 20–21; SGT Daniel Schroeder:
pp. 36–37; TSgt Jacob N. Bailey: pp. 30–31;
Dreamstime: Mpwood: p. 1; Getty Images:
pp. 8–9, 28–29, 35, 40–41; AFP: pp. 32–33,
34, 38–39; Time & Life Pictures: pp. 24–25;
US Navy – edited version © Science
Faction: pp. 16–17; White-Thomson
Publishing/Stefan Chabluk: pp. 25, 38;
Wikimedia: p. 7; U.S. Navy photo by Mass
Communication Specialist 2nd Class
William S. Parker: front cover;
www.sealswcc.com: pp. 3, 44–45.

Library and Archives Canada Cataloguing in Publication

Bow, James, 1972-
    Navy SEALs / James Bow.

(Crabtree chrome)
Includes index.
Issued also in electronic formats.
ISBN 978-0-7787-7926-1 (bound).--ISBN 978-0-7787-7935-3
(pbk.)

    1. United States. Navy. SEALs--Juvenile literature. I. Title.
II. Series: Crabtree chrome

VG87.B69 2012   j359.9'84   C2012-907045-9

Library of Congress Cataloging-in-Publication Data

Bow, James.
    Navy SEALs / James Bow.
       p. cm. -- (Crabtree chrome)
    Includes index.
    Audience: Ages 11-14.
    ISBN 978-0-7787-7926-1 (library binding : alk. paper) -- ISBN
978-0-7787-7935-3 (pbk. : alk. paper) -- ISBN 978-1-4271-7856-5
(electronic pdf) -- ISBN 978-1-4271-7871-5 (electronic html)
    1. United States. Navy. SEALs--Juvenile literature. 2. United
States. Navy--Commando troops--Juvenile literature. I. Title.

VG87.B69 2013
359.9'84--dc23
                                      2012041844

Printed in the U.S.A./112012/FA20121012

Published in Canada
Crabtree Publishing
616 Welland Ave.
St. Catharines, ON
L2M 5V6

Published in the United States
Crabtree Publishing
PMB 59051
350 Fifth Avenue, 59th Floor
New York, New York 10118

Published in the United Kingdom
Crabtree Publishing
Maritime House
Basin Road North, Hove
BN41 1WR

Published in Australia
Crabtree Publishing
3 Charles Street
Coburg North
VIC 3058

Contents

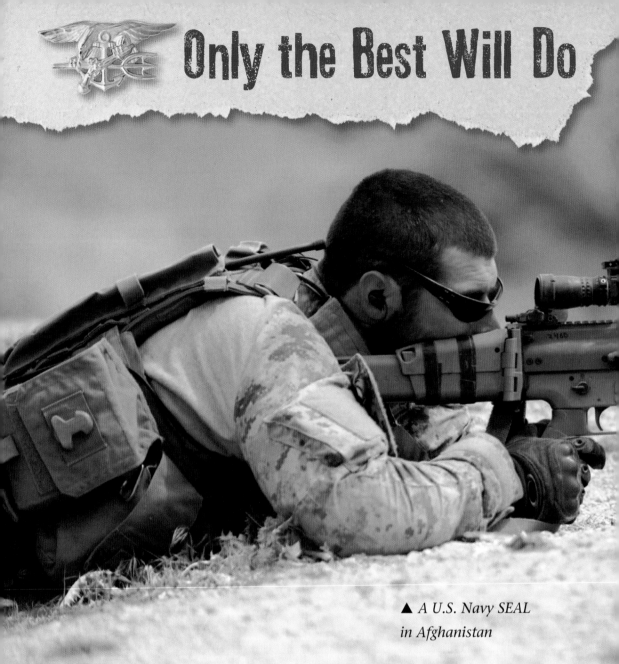

▲ *A U.S. Navy SEAL in Afghanistan*

Waiting for the Order

In the dark of night, 79 Navy SEAL commandos wait
on board two helicopters. Their guns are at their
sides. Their equipment is in their packs. They think
over the mission to come. They've trained for this,
they know what they must do, and they are ready.
But they still have to wait for the order to come.

At Last!

Finally, the order comes. The helicopters power up. Soldiers shout over the roar of the blades. When all is ready, the helicopters lift off. The SEALs on board are calm as they head into their deadly mission: to kill **terrorist** leader Osama Bin Laden.

Navy SEALs are an elite group of soldiers who conduct "special warfare." This includes raids. Small groups are sent behind enemy lines to make small but deadly attacks, to hurt the enemy and rescue people.

 terrorist: someone who uses violence to get what they want.

Before the SEALs

During World War II, the U.S. military set up a group called the Navy Scouts and Raiders, to land unseen in enemy territory and set up markers to help American soldiers land from the sea. If the scouts were caught by the enemy, there would be no one who could help them.

▼ *SEAL stands for Sea, Air, and Land Teams.*

▲ *United States Navy Special Warfare Command badge*

Navy SEALs

Since 1962, the United States government has used Navy SEALs to creep up on the enemy and defeat or disarm them without hurting **civilians**.

Phil Bucklew is called "the father of naval special warfare." He led the Navy Scouts and Raiders on landings in Italy, southern France, and Normandy. When the Navy SEALs formed in 1962, he was their first commander.

civilians: people who are not part of the military.

The First SEALs

In 1961, the U.S. was fighting in the Vietnam War. They were fighting a group of soldiers called the Viet Cong who used **guerrilla tactics**. Many U.S. soldiers were killed. President Kennedy remembered the work the special forces had done during World War II. He decided to use specially trained soldiers who could fight from sea, air, or land. These were the first Navy SEALs.

◀ Using camouflage helped the SEALs to hide in the Vietnamese jungle.

The Men with Green Faces

The SEALs fought the Viet Cong and stopped enemy supplies from getting through. The Viet Cong were successful because they had used the jungle to hide and make surprise attacks. The SEALs did the same thing. They painted their faces green so they would be camouflaged in the jungle. The Viet Cong called them "the men with green faces."

▼ *SEALs land in South Vietnam, 1967*

The SEALs fought hard in Vietnam. Their skill and bravery was recognized by the U.S. military and they were awarded more medals for their service than most other groups of soldiers in the war.

 guerrilla tactics: fighting with small groups using sneak attacks.

9

Picking the Best

A Navy SEAL must be between 18 and 28 years old. He must be a U.S. citizen and already be a member of the U.S. Navy. Sailors already know how to fight at sea. But sailors who want to be SEALs have to prove they can be strong under the toughest conditions. It takes up to 30 months of hard training before a Navy SEAL is sent on a mission.

▲ *A SEAL candidate tackles an obstacle course as part of his initial training.*

Got What it Takes?

SEAL **candidates** must be able to swim 500 yards (457 meters) in less than 12.5 minutes. They have to be able to do 42 push-ups and 50 sit-ups in four minutes. After six pull-ups, they must be able to run 1.5 miles (2.4 kilometers) in under 11.5 minutes, and all of this within an hour. Pass the test, and the real training can begin.

Only men are allowed to join the Navy SEALs. Some women serve in U.S. special forces units as information specialists.

 candidates: people who apply for a job.

Basic Training

SEALs are trained in hard combat. Early in their training, they do Basic Underwater Demolition/SEAL (BUD/S). For seven months, they learn how to fight underwater and how to blow things up. SEALs are tested on their **stamina** and how well they work under pressure. In real combat, they will have to fight the enemy in the toughest of conditions.

Some Don't Make It

The hardest part of this training is called "Hell Week." SEAL candidates dive, land, search and destroy as if they are in real combat. They do this for five and a half days without sleeping. Candidates can quit at any time, and eight out of every ten don't finish the course. The Navy expects this—they want the best of the best.

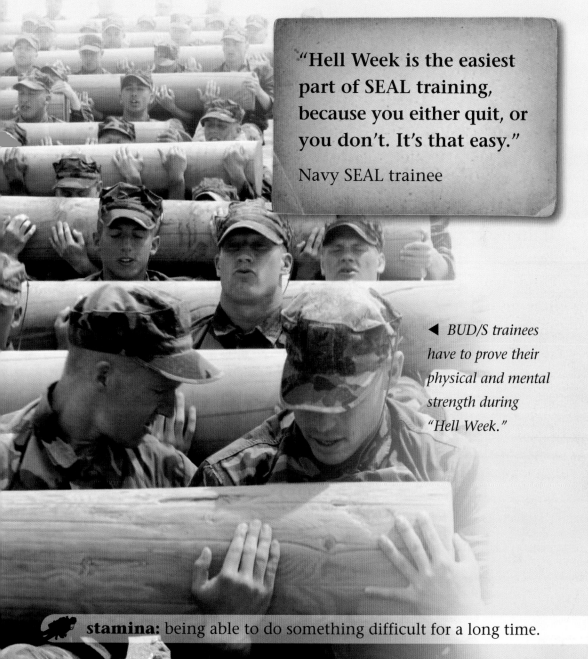

"**Hell Week is the easiest part of SEAL training, because you either quit, or you don't. It's that easy.**"

Navy SEAL trainee

◄ *BUD/S trainees have to prove their physical and mental strength during "Hell Week."*

stamina: being able to do something difficult for a long time.

▼ *BUD/S trainees take part in "surf passage" training in a small inflatable boat.*

Special Skills

If they successfully complete BUD/S, candidates learn next how to find their way in the wilderness. They learn how to skydive, and how to fight in small spaces. They learn how to use weapons, and how to fight without them. They also learn medical skills. These are just some of the special skills that make the Navy SEALs a powerful force.

Combat Ready

But the most important thing SEALs learn is teamwork. For the next 18 months, they're assigned to a platoon (a group of soldiers led by a commander). Everybody gets to know each other. Fighting deep in enemy territory, the only people a SEAL can count on are the other men in his platoon. This time together helps build this trust.

"The only easy day was yesterday."

SEAL **motto**

 motto: a sentence to express someone's beliefs or ideals.

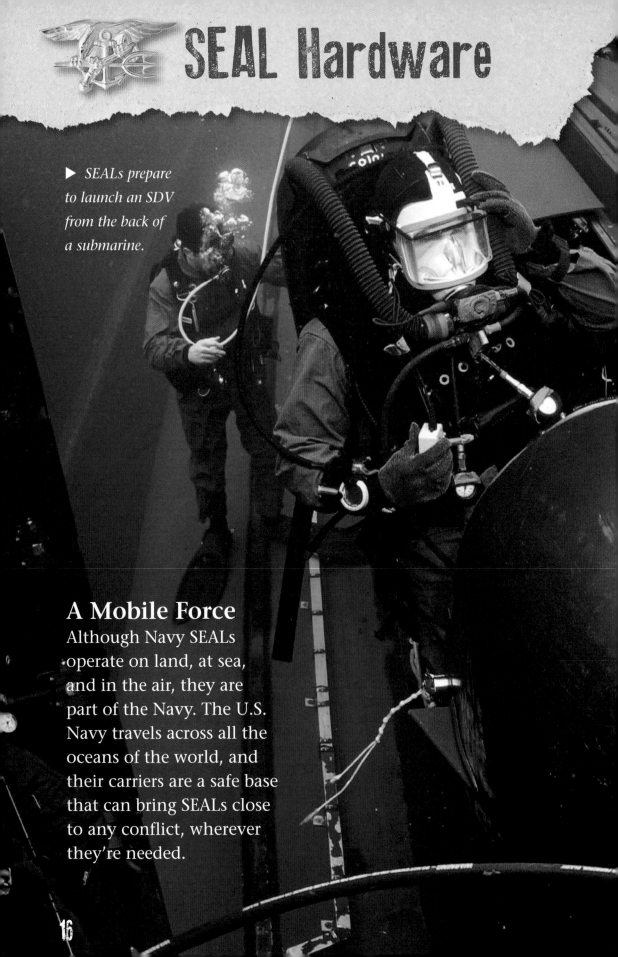

SEAL Hardware

▶ *SEALs prepare to launch an SDV from the back of a submarine.*

A Mobile Force

Although Navy SEALs operate on land, at sea, and in the air, they are part of the Navy. The U.S. Navy travels across all the oceans of the world, and their carriers are a safe base that can bring SEALs close to any conflict, wherever they're needed.

Speedy Delivery

From navy ships, **submersible** SEAL Delivery Vehicles (SDVs) can bring SEALs ashore under the water. SEALs can then surface for a surprise attack. For faster landings, SEALs use Special Operations Craft. These speedboats rush across the water to their targets. For missions inland, Black Hawk helicopters fly low, swoop in, and deliver the SEALs often before the enemy knows they are on the way.

The Black Hawk helicopters that were used in the hunt for Osama Bin Laden (see page 28) had special technology to keep them from being spotted by enemy RADAR.

submersible: a vehicle or anything that can work underwater.

Fighting Light

SEALs are able to fight without weapons, but they need guns for their missions. They prefer weapons that are light, small, and accurate. This helps them move quickly and work in small spaces. They use Heckler & Koch carbine military **assault** rifles and also handguns. The SEALs have combat knives for hand-to-hand fighting.

▼ *This Navy SEAL is armed with an assault rifle equipped with a grenade launcher.*

Prepared for Anything

If Navy SEALs meet enemy vehicles such as planes or tanks, they're prepared. The FIM-92 Stinger is an easy-to-carry rocket launcher that can take down enemy helicopters. The M136 AT4 is a gun that can pierce the armor of a tank. SEALs can carry these into battle, and fire them using their shoulder to support the gun.

Navy SEALs are also trained in unarmed combat. SEALs can learn a number of martial arts to take down the enemy quickly and, most importantly, quietly.

 assault: to attack.

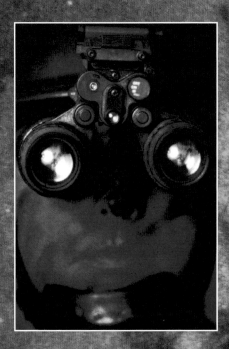

SEAL Armor

Navy SEALs wear protective vests and helmets made from a very strong woven fabric that can stop a bullet where metal can't. SEAL officers tend not to use heavy armored vehicles, however. They want to be able to move quickly.

▶ *This night-vision photo shows Navy SEALs in Kandahar province, Afghanistan.*

Seeing Eyes

Navy SEALs don't go in blind on night missions. Night-vision goggles help SEALs see in the dark. Infrared cameras can see body heat. X-ray cameras can see through walls. With these tools, SEALs can see hidden enemy soldiers, waiting to attack, or a hidden entrance to an enemy base.

We can't tell you much about the equipment the SEALs use because a lot of it is **classified**. Secrets give armies an advantage.

 classified: when something is kept secret by the government.

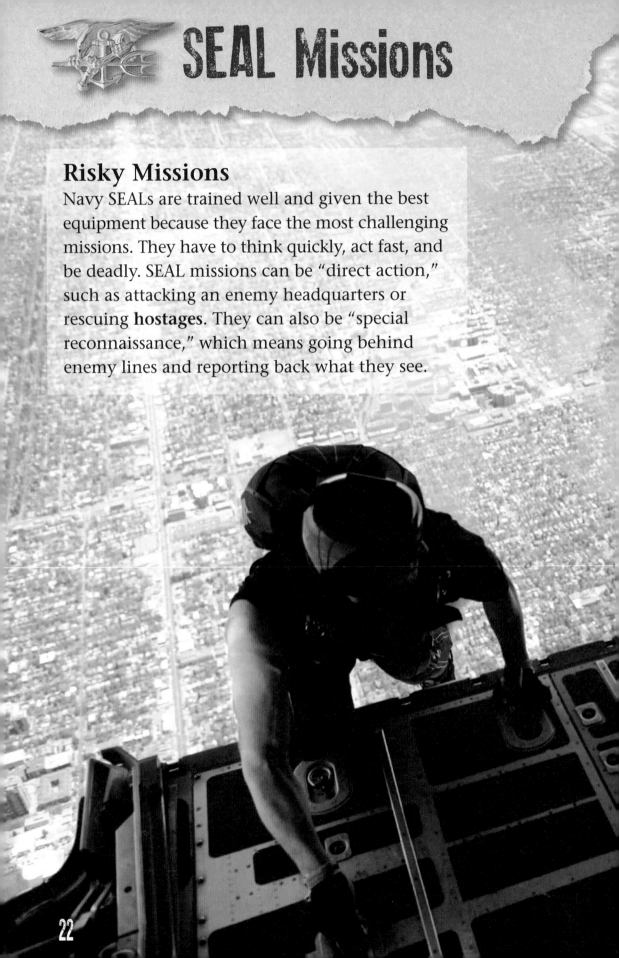

SEAL Missions

Risky Missions

Navy SEALs are trained well and given the best equipment because they face the most challenging missions. They have to think quickly, act fast, and be deadly. SEAL missions can be "direct action," such as attacking an enemy headquarters or rescuing **hostages**. They can also be "special reconnaissance," which means going behind enemy lines and reporting back what they see.

Counter-Terrorism

SEALs fight against terrorists. This is called counter-terrorism. Terrorist tactics include doing damage by secretly planting bombs and explosives. A terrorist group might hide out among civilians, so attacking the terrorists could mean innocent people are killed. But Navy SEALs know how to scout in small groups and make quick, targeted strikes to keep the number of injured to a minimum.

◀ *Two Navy SEALs prepare to jump out of a Hercules aircraft.*

The Navy SEALs have **trained** other countries' militaries on how to use special forces.

 hostages: people who are held against their will.

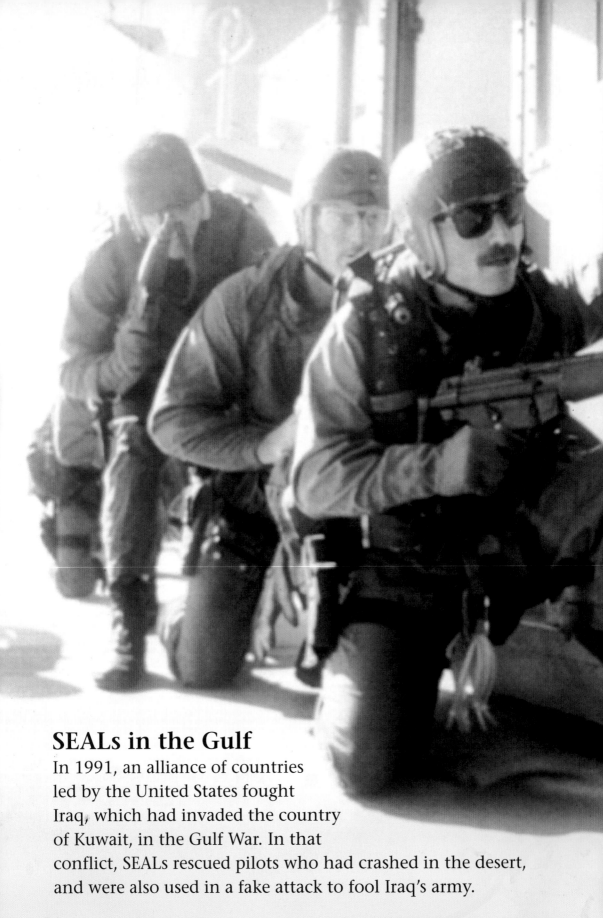

SEALs in the Gulf

In 1991, an alliance of countries
led by the United States fought
Iraq, which had invaded the country
of Kuwait, in the Gulf War. In that
conflict, SEALs rescued pilots who had crashed in the desert,
and were also used in a fake attack to fool Iraq's army.

◀ *SEALs perform a training exercise during the Gulf War.*

Fake Attack

Just as the war started, SEALs landed on a beach in Kuwait. They set off explosives and fired guns, making the Iraqi army think the alliance was invading by sea. The **diversion** worked. Iraqi soldiers moved toward the sea to fight, which meant their forces were weaker when the real invasion came instead from Saudi Arabia.

▲ *Iraq invaded Kuwait in the 1990–91 Gulf War.*

In January 2012, SEALs swooped into a heavily guarded hideout in Somalia and rescued two hostages held by pirates.

 diversion: a distraction from something more important.

Sometimes Things Go Wrong

When the U.S. invaded the Caribbean island of Grenada in 1983, the SEALs were told to capture the island's radio tower. One of the SEALs' boats **capsized**, killing four men. When they got to the tower, the SEALs' own radio wouldn't work. Surrounded by the enemy, unable to radio for help, the SEALs fought their way back to the water, and made it out alive.

Helicopter Down

In 2011, in Afghanistan, fighters from an enemy called the Taliban shot down a Chinook helicopter bringing reinforcements to the U.S. Army near Kabul. Twenty-two Navy SEALs died. This was the biggest loss suffered by U.S. special forces in over 25 years. SEALs are well aware what can go wrong when they go on a mission. They go anyway.

◀ *The helicopter shot down by the Taliban in Afghanistan in 2011 was a Chinook, like this one.*

"I never lost any men while they were with me."

Phil Bucklew, SEAL Commander

capsized: flipped over in the water.

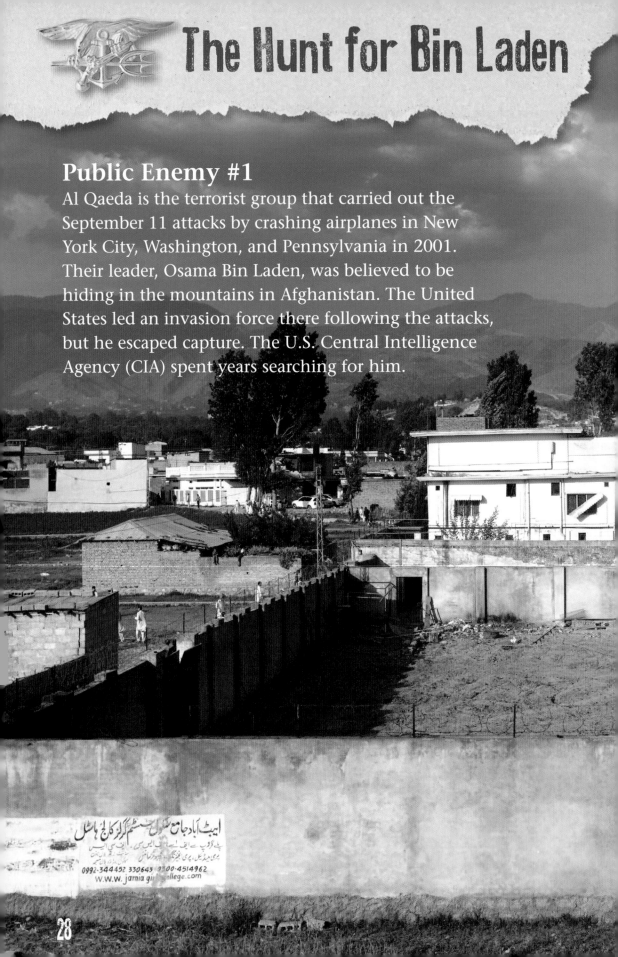

Public Enemy #1

Al Qaeda is the terrorist group that carried out the September 11 attacks by crashing airplanes in New York City, Washington, and Pennsylvania in 2001. Their leader, Osama Bin Laden, was believed to be hiding in the mountains in Afghanistan. The United States led an invasion force there following the attacks, but he escaped capture. The U.S. Central Intelligence Agency (CIA) spent years searching for him.

Only the SEALs Would Do

In January 2011, the CIA learned that Bin Laden was living in a **compound** in Abbottabad, Pakistan. To capture Bin Laden, soldiers would have to sneak into the compound, strike fast, and leave quickly. Clearly, this was a job for the Navy SEALs.

▼ *The target was Osama Bin Laden's compound in Abbottabad, Pakistan.*

The U.S. military couldn't use stealth bombers to kill Bin Laden. Abbottabad was a city of 60,000 and an air strike would have also killed Pakistani civilians. The U.S. government wanted to take him in person to prove they actually had captured Bin Laden.

 compound: a building or area enclosed by a barrier.

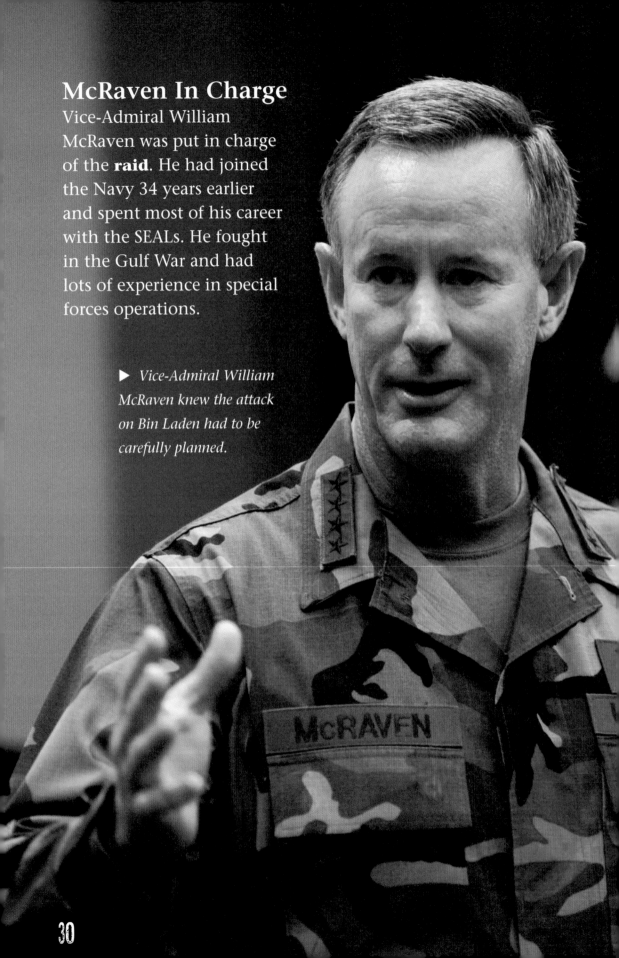

McRaven In Charge

Vice-Admiral William McRaven was put in charge of the **raid**. He had joined the Navy 34 years earlier and spent most of his career with the SEALs. He fought in the Gulf War and had lots of experience in special forces operations.

▶ *Vice-Admiral William McRaven knew the attack on Bin Laden had to be carefully planned.*

Making Plans

McRaven knew the force to capture Bin Laden had to be small and work fast, and it had to come in from far away. McRaven worried that if he worked with the Pakistani military, Bin Laden might hear of the operation and flee. The SEAL team would have to fly in from Afghanistan without the knowledge of the Pakistan government.

> McRaven considered using B-2 bombers to destroy the compound. He also considered a joint raid with Pakistani forces. In the end, he felt he could only trust the SEALs to do it right.

raid: a quick and precise attack on a target in enemy territory.

▼ *Bin Laden's compound was stocked with weapons and food, even cases of Coca Cola and Pepsi. It was clear he could hold out for a while.*

Red Squadron

McRaven put together a team from Red **Squadron**, a group of SEALs who were coming home to the United States from Afghanistan. They had worked in Pakistan and knew the local languages. At first, the team members weren't told what their mission was. They rehearsed parts of the operation twice in the United States before returning to Afghanistan.

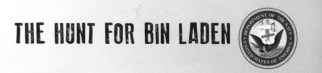

Expecting the Worst

McRaven kept his plan flexible. He made a plan in case Bin Laden surrendered, and one in case the Pakistani military caught the SEALs. Backup helicopters were to be kept ready nearby, in case the SEALs had to fight their way out.

"This is what we do. We fly in by helicopters, we assault compounds, we grab the bad guy or whatever is required, and we get out."

Admiral McRaven to President Obama

squadron: an air force unit of two or more aircraft.

Dress Rehearsal

In Afghanistan, the SEALs practiced at a full-scale replica, or copy, of Bin Laden's compound. Chain-link fences were used to mark building positions and walls instead of concrete. This caused problems later, but it helped the SEALs understand where to attack and how to move.

▲ *This model of the compound was once top secret. It took six weeks to build and was used to plan the mission to capture Bin Laden.*

Briefing the President

McRaven **briefed** President Obama and his military advisors. Obama asked if McRaven was sure the plan would work. McRaven said his team was ready, and the conditions were right. Obama wished McRaven well, and thanked the SEALs for their service. The SEALs finally discovered who their target was.

"They were told, 'We think we found Osama bin Laden, and your job is to kill him.' The SEALs started to cheer."

Officer who briefed the SEALs

▼ *President Obama discusses the mission with National Security Advisor Tom Donilon.*

MR. DONI

 briefed: told somebody all they needed to know about something.

▲ *The Navy SEALs flew in two Black Hawk helicopters.*

79 Commandos and a Dog

The plan was for 24 Navy SEALs to fly in two helicopters to attack Bin Laden's compound. The team included pilots, navigators, and **intelligence** gatherers. Another 49 SEALs stayed behind in Afghanistan, ready to fly in if the attack went badly. Six officers commanded the mission back at the air base.

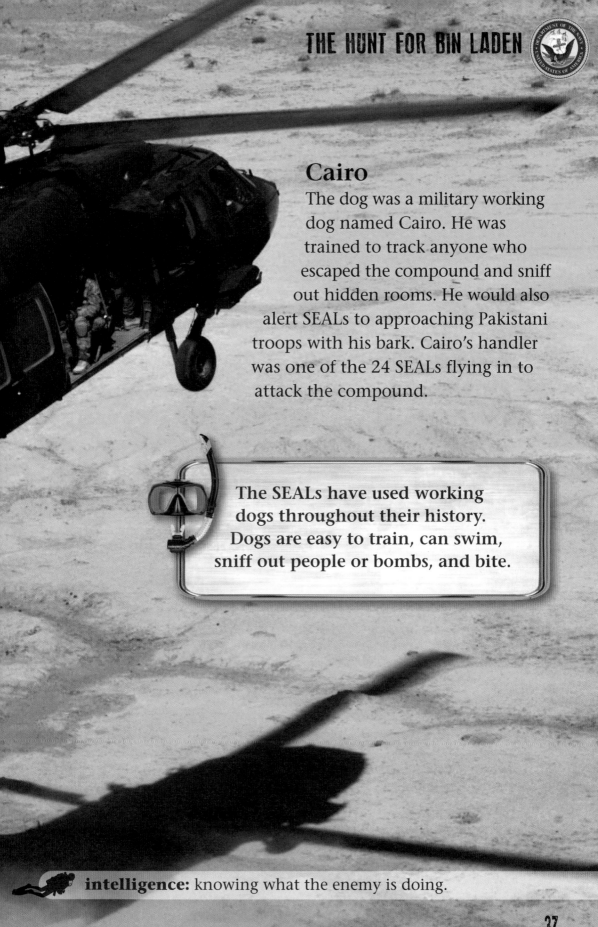

Cairo

The dog was a military working dog named Cairo. He was trained to track anyone who escaped the compound and sniff out hidden rooms. He would also alert SEALs to approaching Pakistani troops with his bark. Cairo's handler was one of the 24 SEALs flying in to attack the compound.

The SEALs have used working dogs throughout their history. Dogs are easy to train, can swim, sniff out people or bombs, and bite.

intelligence: knowing what the enemy is doing.

Going In!

The Order Comes

Finally, on May 1, 2011, at 1:22 p.m. Eastern Time, the order comes to attack. In Abbottabad, it is the darkest part of the night. The helicopters take off from Afghanistan, 186 miles (300 km) away. Using night-vision goggles, pilots fly the Black Hawks low over the hilly ground, keeping out of sight.

▲ *Abbottabad is a city in the northeast of Pakistan,*
31 miles (50 km) from the capital Islamabad.

Not All Goes Well

At 2:52 p.m. Bin Laden's compound comes into view. One helicopter hovers over the courtyard as the SEALs prepare to attack. But there's a problem: the high walls of the compound (concrete rather than chain-link fence) create a bad wind against the helicopter's rotor blades. This makes it impossible for the helicopter to fly, and it falls. The SEALs on board **brace** for the crash.

◀ *The city of Abbottabad lies in a valley surrounded by hills.*

President Obama and other government officials watched live updates of the operation in the White House Situation Room.

brace: prepare for a big hit.

▼ *The helicopter crash-landed in this courtyard. The SEALS blew up t* *helicopter to keep the secret technology from falling into enemy hands.*

Crash!

Amazingly, nobody on the crashed helicopter is hurt. The SEALs grab their weapons and the mission carries on. The second helicopter lands outside and the SEALs scale the outside walls. Using explosives to **breach** walls and blow down doors, the SEALs rush into the compound.

Room to Room

The SEALs find people just waking up. The SEALs go room to room, pinning people down, searching for their target. Anybody with a gun is shot. Finally, reaching the third floor, they burst into a bedroom and find Bin Laden and three of his wives.

There were 22 people in the compound: four men, five women, and 13 children. All four men, which included Bin Laden and one of his adult sons, were killed. One of the women was also killed, but none of the children.

breach: blow apart using explosives.

Geronimo! Geronimo! Geronimo!

One woman shouts Bin Laden's name and charges the SEALs. A SEAL shoots her in the leg. A second SEAL shoots Bin Laden in the chest and the head. With Bin Laden dead, the team sends a radio message to headquarters: "For God and country— Geronimo, Geronimo, Geronimo!" This code tells them that the mission is a success.

In and Out

The SEALs handcuff the women and children, grab weapons and search the compound for information. They destroy as much of the crashed helicopter as they can to stop the technology from falling into enemy hands. The SEALs take Bin Laden's body and fly away. The mission was planned to take 40 minutes. It was done in 38. It would go down in history as one of the most famous Navy SEAL missions of all time.

▶ *Secretary of State Hillary Clinton described watching the events from the Situation Room as "The most **intense** 38 minutes of my life."*

After making sure the body was that of Bin Laden, the U.S. Navy buried him at sea.

intense: extremely strong or forceful.

43

For God and Country

There are 2,500 active SEALs in the Navy. They usually serve for six years, and many go back to regular duties after their time as a SEAL. The hard training and the amount of time they are away from home are burdens they can carry only for so long. But the pride and honor of the SEALs stay with all who serve. They know they're brave enough, strong enough, and have the skills to do what their country calls for them to do.

Looking Ahead

New technology like robot planes, better armor, and lighter weapons will make the Navy SEALs' fight easier. But as technology improves to help the SEALs fight, the SEALs will be expected to take on more complicated missions. Navy SEALs will keep training hard, fighting hard, and making split-second decisions **under fire**.

◄ *The SEALs will continue to prepare for any mission that calls for their special skills.*

"You are, literally, the finest small-fighting force that has ever existed in the world."

President Obama to the SEALs team

 under fire: when people are being shot at.

Books

The Navy SEALs by Jennifer M. Besel (Capstone, 2011)

U.S. Navy Special Forces: SEAL Teams by Michael Burgan (Capstone, 2000)

Armed Forces: Navy SEALs by Jack David (Bellwether Media, 2009)

The U.S. Navy SEALs at War by Michael Green and Gladys Green (Capstone High-Interest, 2004)

Navy SEALs by Drew Nelson (Gareth Stevens Pub., 2012)

Websites

www.sealswcc.com/ The official Navy SEALs website.

www.navysealmuseum.com/ National Navy UDT-SEAL Museum.

http://science.howstuff works.com/ navy-seal.htm How the Navy SEALs work.

www.navysealfoundation.org Navy SEAL Foundation.

Movies

Quote from *www.usnavyseals.com*: "There are very few great films that capture the spirit and heart of the United States Navy SEALs. Many films feature mentions of the Navy SEALs in some regard, but fail to focus their entire films on these great individuals."

Navy SEALs—A 1990 film directed by Lewis Teague and starring Charlie Sheen.

G.I. Jane—A 1997 film by Ridley Scott presenting the idea of a woman training for the Navy SEALs.

Glossary

assault To attack

brace Prepare for a big hit

breach Blow apart using explosives

briefed Told somebody all they needed to know about something

candidates People who apply for a job

capsized Flipped over in the water

civilians People who are not part of the military

classified When something is kept secret by the government

compound A building or area enclosed by a barrier

diversion: A distraction from something more important

guerrilla tactics Fighting with small groups using sneak attacks

hostages: People who are held against their will

intelligence Knowing what the enemy is doing

intense Extremely strong or forceful

motto A sentence to express someone's beliefs or ideals

raid A quick and precise attack on a target in enemy territory

squadron An air force unit of two or more aircraft

stamina Being able to do something difficult for a long time

submersible A vehicle or anything that can work underwater

terrorist Someone who uses violence to get what they want

under fire When people are being shot at

Index

Entries in **bold** refer to pictures